COASTAL SHIPPING
The Twilight Years

Ian Collard

Polish Shipping Line *Skrzat* (1961, 999grt) leaves Waterloo Dock in Liverpool. She was sold to Finnish shipbreakers and arrived at Hamina on 17 October 1984.

COASTAL SHIPPING
The Twilight Years

Ian Collard

TEMPUS

Hispania, a Swedish Lloyd vessel (1966, 7,772grt, 141m x 21m, 18 knots). She was built as the *Svea* and became the *Hispania* in 1969. She was renamed *Saga* in 1972, *Knossos* in 1978 and *Captain Zaman II* in 1998.

First published 2000
Reprinted 2004

Tempus Publishing Limited
The Mill, Brimscombe Port,
Stroud, Gloucestershire, GL5 2QG
www.tempus-publishing.com

British Library Cataloguing in Publication Data.
A catalogue record for this book is available from the British Library.

ISBN 0 7524 1768 1

Typesetting and origination by Tempus Publishing Limited.
Printed in Great Britain.

Contents

Acknowledgements

I wish to thank all of the shipping companies that have provided me with information and details of ships they have owned, as well as the various port authorities which have allowed me to photograph the vessels shown in the book. Without their valuable help and assistance it would not have been possible to compile this work.

Scottish Coast of Burns & Laird (1957, 3,817grt, 104m x 16m, 17 knots). Sold to Greek owners in 1969, she was renamed *Galaxias*. She retained this name for twenty years and became the *Princesa Amorosa* in 1989.

Introduction

The 1960s saw the demise of the conventional coastal passenger vessel and its replacement by the purpose-built car ferry. People wished to take their cars with them when they travelled abroad for business and pleasure, and operators were forced to respond to the changing needs of the traveller.

Some shipping companies converted vessels into car carriers, which gave welcome business to shipbuilders and repairers who began to specialize in this type of work. Other operators resisted change and attempted to carry on with ships that were totally inadequate for the demands of the changing market.

There were operators with vision who, a decade earlier, had designed and built car ferries, and could now cope with the new demands made on them. It became clear that the holiday and leisure industry was changing dramatically and change was needed for some shipping companies to survive.

The world was becoming smaller with the introduction of the package holiday and the increase in the number of people willing to fly to their destination rather than travel by sea and overland by train or coach. This was the first generation to break with tradition and holiday in the Mediterranean or Atlantic Islands rather than Rothesay, Southend or Douglas, Isle of Man.

It was also impossible to escape the effects of unpredictable world markets, especially when attempting to plan for the future – oil prices were rising virtually every week. Some services became unprofitable, and it was no longer viable to operate them. Employment opportunities were affected and local communities were threatened with a reduction in, or loss of, services that had sometimes operated for many years.

However, the introduction of new vessels on traditional routes proved very successful and profitable for most shipping operators and they increased the size of their fleets as larger vessels with improved facilities were introduced. New routes were opened, which quickly became popular, providing employment for local communities and profit for the operators.

It was the beginning of a vast rebuilding programme in the major coastal ports, which culminated the construction of two-tier berths which enabled ships to turn around more quickly. Speed was important on routes where fierce competition existed. Some vessels were built which were capable of 23 knots to enable the operator to advertise a reduced journey time.

Some vessels which had given their owners a profitable return over the years were disposed of to the breakers yard and others found new employment in warmer climes. The Greek shipping industry was expanding at the time and owners were anxious to acquire good quality, reliable and economical vessels.

The development of the British motorway system was responsible for taking a substantial amount of cargo from the coastal freight network operated by many small and medium-sized companies. Cargo was transhipped from the main ports by coastal freighter to ports around the coastline of the British Isles and Europe.

Most cargo was carried in vessels designed in the traditional manner and the introduction of containerization caused a complete revolution across the shipping industry. Roll on/roll off vessels were introduced which enabled operators and the road transport industry to develop a strategy to increase the amount of freight carried.

By the end of the decade most operators were in the process of replacing their fleets with new roll on/roll off passenger and freight vessels, while port authorities were responding by providing modern facilities. The new ferries were larger and more luxurious than their predecessors, and contained shops, restaurants, lounges and amusement arcades. They set the standard for the super-ferries which were to follow and provided some well overdue improvements for the travelling public.

At the beginning of the twenty-first century, many coastal resemble mini liners and incorporate features one would never have anticipated back in the 1960s. Speed is now an important factor and operators have introduced high speed mono hulls and catamarans to their fleets. They operate at around 40 knots in ideal circumstances and can halve journey times on many routes.

The coastal passenger and freight vessel plays an important part in the life of many local communities. The Scottish Highlands and Islands rely on a good ferry service to provide a regular and reliable link with the mainland. The other island communities of the British Isles also find that the ferry is an important element of any integrated transport system.

In the 1960s the ferry services across the English Channel provided the link with other European ports and the main way goods and passengers were transported in bulk. Most of the ports and operators took advantage of their position and invested in their facilities. It is now a time of rationalization with the opening of the Channel Tunnel and the operation of a rail service transporting passengers, freight and cars to the heart of Europe.

Most of the ferries will be fondly remembered by people who travelled on them, and their contribution to the development of regions across the British Isles cannot be underestimated. Some gave sterling service in times of war, while others provided a bridge between the mainland and isolated communities.

Many of the vessels shown in this book have now been replaced by newer ships, although some are still employed sailing around the Greek Islands. They have served their owners well and have given good service to the industry and the public. They provided an efficient and convenient way of transporting goods and vehicles by sea, and transformed the image of sea travel by their size, luxury and range of facilities on board.

One

Channel Ports

Dover is the main Channel port. In the 1960s services were operated by British Railways, the Belgium Marine Administration, the Societe National des Chemins de Fer Francais (SNCF) and Townsend Car Ferries.

There were regular sailings to Calais, Boulogne, Zeebrugge and Ostend provided by car ferries, train ferries, hovercraft and the few conventional passenger vessels that remained in service. Services to Dieppe, Calais and Boulogne were also operated from Folkestone and Newhaven. British Railways provided freight and passenger services from Weymouth to the Channel Islands.

Normandy Ferries and Thoreson Car Ferries provided sailings from Southampton to France, and it was also possible to take a mini cruise from Southampton to Spain aboard the Swedish Lloyd Line vessels *Hispania* (1966/7772grt) and *Patricia* (1967/8897grt).

The short sea route to the Isle of Wight was the responsibility of the Southampton, Isle of Wight Steam Packet Company, who operated with a fleet of modern car ferries. British Railways Isle of Wight services ran from Portsmouth to Rye and Fishbourne and Lymington to Yarmouth.

Falaise of British Railways (1947, 3,710grt, 95m x 15m, 20½ knots). She was sold to Spanish shipbreakers and left Holyhead in tow for Bilbao on 24 December 1974.

An SNCF vessel, *Villandry* (1965, 3,445grt 105m x 18m, 21 knots). In 1985 she became the *Olympia* and in 1986 was renamed *Delos*. She was broken up in India in 1996.

Valencay, another SNCF vessel (1965, 3,477grt, 105m x 17m, 21 knots). In 1985 she was sold to the Greeks and was renamed *Eptanisos*.

The Dover Harbour Board's *Diligent* (1957, 161grt). In 1985 she was sold to Frank Pearce, who resold her to S&H Towage. In 1990 she was again resold and became the *Omni St Laurent*.

Dover, British Railways (1965, 3,602grt 112m x 17m 19½knots). She was renamed *Earl Siward* in 1977, *Sol Express* in 1982 and was berthed on the River Tyne as the *Tuxedo Royale* in 1986. On 31 March 2000 she arrived at Middlesbrough Dock, towed by the tug *Jerome Letzer*. She is to be berthed at No.11 Quay as a nightclub and restaurant.

Lord Warden, British Railways (1952, 3,333grt 110m x 18m 20 knots). In 1979 she became the *Al Zaher* and was broken up at Gadani Beach in 1981.

Maid of Kent, another British Railways vessel (1959, 3,920grt, 114m x 18m 20½ knots). She was broken up at San Esteban De Pravia where she arrived on 21 April 1982.

This British Railways vessel, *Vortigan*, (1969, 4,371grt, 115m x 19m, 20 knots)was sold in 1988 and renamed *Milos Express*.

Normannia of British Railways (1952, 3,543grt, 94m x 15m 19½knots). She was broken up at Gijon in Spain, arriving there from Newhaven on 6 December 1978.

British Railways' *Invicta* (1940, 4,191grt, 117m x 15m, 22 knots). She left Newhaven on 21 September 1972 under tow, bound for Rotterdam where she was broken up.

Hampton Ferry (1934, 2,989grt) and *Reine Astrid* (1958, 3,794grt) at Dover. *Hampton Ferry* became the *Tre Arddur* in 1971 and arrived at Valencia on 5 July 1973 to be broken up.

Twickenham Ferry of British Railways (1934, 2,839grt, 106m x 19m 16½ knots). She was sold to Steelnorte at San Esteban De Pravia for breaking up, arriving there on 26 May 1974.

British Railways' *Shepperton Ferry* (1935, 2,996grt 106m x 19m 16½ knots). She arrived at Bilbao, Spain, from Dover on 17 September 1972, for demolition by Hierros Ardes S.A.

Norfolk Ferry of British Railways (1951, 3,137grt, 122m x 18m, 13 knots). She was broken up in Ouderkerk, Holland in 1983.

Rio Leopold III of Belgium State Marine (1956, 3,794grt 114m x 15m, 23 knots). She was sold and renamed *Najd* in 1978 and broken up in Pakistan in 1987.

Koningen Elisabeth, also of Belgium State Marine (1957, 3,594grt 114m x 15m, 22 knots). She was renamed *Abha* in 1978, *Najd II* in 1979 and broken up at Eleusis in Greece in 1984.

Belgium State Marine Dover-Ostend and
Harwich-Ostend leaflets.

Roi Baudouin of Belgium State Marine (1965, 3,241grt 118m x 16m, 21 knots). She was sold in 1982 and renamed *Georgios Express*.

Princesse Astrid, another Belgium State Marine vessel (1968, 3,148grt, 117m x 16m, 22 knots). She became the *Bari Express* in 1983 and the *Express Hermes* in 1998.

Artevelde of Belgium State Marine (1958, 2,812grt 117m x 15m, 21 knots). She was renamed *Aigaion* in 1976.

Reine Astrid, Belgium State Marine (1958, 3,794grt, 114m x 15m, 22 knots). This vessel was converted to Jetfoil Terminal at Dover in 1983.

Belgium State Marine's *Prinses Paola* (1966, 4,356grt, 117m x 16m, 24 knots). She was sold and renamed *Tropicana* in 1988. She became *Sea Palace* in 1990, *Saint Lucie* in 1991 and *Tropicana* again in 1994.

Koningen Fabiola of Belgium State Marine (1962, 3,745grt, 117m x 16m 22 knots). She was renamed *Olympia* and *Lydia* in 1985, *Ephesus* in 1995, *Bergama* in 1996 and *Bosporus* in 1998.

Seaspeed SRN 4 Mark III hovercraft *The Princess Margaret* sails from Dover to Boulogne. She is 330grt and was built in 1968. In 1979 she was lengthened. She was withdrawn from service on 1 October 2000.

Free Enterprise V of Townsend Car Ferries (1970, 5,044grt 118m x 20m, 21 knots). She was renamed *Pride of Hythe* in 1987, then sold in 1993 and renamed *Laburnum*.

A rough winter crossing from Dover to Zeebrugge.

Free Enterprise I of Townsend Car Ferries (1962, 2,607grt, 96m x 16m, 18 knots). Having begun her career as *Free Enterprise*, she was renamed many times, becoming *Kimolos* in 1980, *Ergina* in 1993, *Ventouris* in 1994, *Methodia II* in 1995 and *Kallisti* in 1996.

Autocarrier of Townsend Car Ferries (1948, 1,851grt, 91m x 15m, 20 knots). She was built as the *Royal Sovereign*, renamed *Autocarrier* in 1967, and sold to the Società Partenopea di Navigazione, Italy in 1974.

Townsend Car Ferries' *Free Enterprise III* (1966, 4,657grt 117m x 19m, 20 knots). She was sold in 1984 and renamed *Tamira* and *Mona's Isle*, before becoming *Al Fahad* in 1986.

Chantilly of SNCF (1966, 3,400grt, 110m x 18m, 20 knots). On 5 September 1982 she collided with *Cote d'Azur* (1981, 8,479grt) off Calais and was severely damaged forward of the bridge. In 1987 she was sold and renamed *Olympia*. In 1990 she became the *Europa Link*, then the *Baltavia*, before becoming *Al Salam* in 1993.

SNCF's *Cote d'Azur* (1951, 4,037grt, 111m x 15m, 22 knots). She became the *Azur* and *Marie F* in 1973 and was broken up in Murcia, Spain, in 1974.

Compiegne of SNCF (1958, 3,483grt, 115m x 18m, 20 knots). She bore several different names, becoming *Ionian Glory* in 1981, *Queen Vergina* in 1989, *Freedom I* in 1990, *Katarina* in 1994 and *Alamira* in 1998.

Saint Germain, another SNCF vessel (1951, 3,400grt, 116m x 19m 18½knots). On 21 February 1979 she was in collision with the bulk carrier *Artadi* (1963, 14,493grt) on a sailing from Dunkirk to Dover. Two people were killed and there was considerable damage to the ship. In 1988 she was sold and renamed *Germain*, before being broken up in Alang where she arrived on 11 August.

Maid of Orleans of British Railways (1949, 3,777grt, 104m x 15m, 22 knots). She left Newhaven on 6 November 1975 for Santander, Spain where she was broken up.

Maid of Orleans (1949, 3,777grt) and *Maid of Kent* (1959, 3,920grt).

Seaspeed Hovercraft
Dover to Boulogne leaflet.

Dover-Boulogne ⇌ Hovercraft

the fastest
newest
British way
to cross
the channel

SRN 4 Hovercraft *The Princess Anne* sails from Dover to Calais. She was built in 1969 and has a service speed of 60 knots. Her final sailing was the 18.00 Dover to Calais service on 1 October 2000.

The Torpoint ferry operates between Devonport and Torpoint in Cornwall. The three vessels were built in the 1960s and were managed by Cornwall County Council and the Plymouth City Council. The three ferries are *Tamar* (1960), *Lynher* (1961) and *Plym* (1968).

Osborne Castle, Southampton, Isle of Wight Steam Packet (1962, 736grt, 58m x 13m, 14 knots). She was sold in 1978 and became the *Gobelette d'argente*.

Norris Castle, Southampton, Isle of Wight Steam Packet (1968, 734grt, 58m x 13m, 14 knots). Sold in 1994, she was renamed *Lovrjenac*.

Carisbrooke Castle (1959 672 grt, 58m x 13m, 14 knots). After being sold in 1974 and renamed *Città di Meta*, she became *Giglio Espresso Seconda* in 1990 and *Giglio Espresso II* in 1999.

Medina (1931, 347grt) was sold to Lymington Yacht Haven where she arrived on 8 May 1974. In 1993 she became the *Island Pride*.

Viking I of Otto Thoresen (1964, 3,608grt, 99m x 18m, 18½knots). This vessel had a succession of name changes, becoming *Viking Victory* in 1977, *Sun Boat* in 1983, *Caravan* in 1985, *Vasmed* and *Sunny Boat* in 1986, *European Glory* in 1990, *Neptunia* in 1992 and *Media II* in 1993.

Viking II of Otto Thoresen (1964, 3,660grt, 99m x 18m, 18¼ knots). Having begun her career as *Car Ferry Viking II*, she was renamed *Earl William* in 1977, *William* in 1992, *Pearl William* in 1992, *Mar Julia* in 1996 and *Cesme Stern* in 1997. On 16 October 1987, while being used as a floating detention centre at Harwich, she went aground off Shotley and was refloated the same day.

Viking III, also of Otto Thoresen (1965, 3,821grt, 99m x 18m, 18½ knots). In 1983 she was sold and renamed *Terje Vigan*, before becoming *Scandinavia* in 1987, *Fenno Star* in 1991 and *Sandefjord* in 1994.

Townsend Car Ferries' *Free Enterprise II* (1965, 4,122grt, 108m x 18m, 19 knots). She was sold to Greek owners in 1983 and renamed *Moby Blu*.

Patricia of Swedish Lloyd (1967, 8,897grt, 141m x 21m, 18 knots). She had many names, becoming *Stena Oceanica* in 1978, *Stena Saga* in 1979, *Lion Queen* in 1988, *Crown Princess Victoria*, *Crown Princess* and *Pacific Star* in 1990, *Sun Fiesta* in 1993, *Lion Queen* in 1994, *Putri Bintang* in 1997 and *Amusement World* in 1998.

Normandy Car Ferries' 'Civilised ships' Southampton to Le Havre services.

Normandy Ferries' *Leopard* (1968, 6,014grt, 135m x 22m, 19 knots). *Leopard* was sold in 1986 and was renamed *Countess M.*

Southsea of Sealink (1948, 837grt, 61m x 15m, 14½ knots). In 1988 she was laid up at Falmouth and was moved to another lay up berth at Falmouth on 7 May 1992. In 1996 she was sold to Brasspatch Ltd., and was moved to Marchwood on 7 May 1997. On 23 November 1997 she was again moved, this time to Bristol, before going to Newport on 10 February 1999.

Two

North East Ports

North Sea Ferries sailed from Hull to Rotterdam and Zeebrugge and their services were operated by the *Norwave* (1965/3540grt) and the *Norwind* (1966/3692grt). In 1966 Ellerman Wilson Line's vessel *Spero* started a passenger and freight service from Hull to Gothenburg. The service was terminated in 1973 and the vessel sold to Greek owners.

The Danish company DFDS operated between Esbjerg and North Shields and Harwich, with the *England* (1964/8221grt) and the *Winston Churchill* (1967/8658grt). The Norwegian Bergen Line sailed between Stavanger, Bergen and Newcastle, with the *Leda* (1953/6670grt), *Jupiter* (1966/9500grt) and *Venus* (1966/9500grt). The *Jupiter* and *Venus* were jointly owned by Bergen and the Fred Olsen Line who operated them on cruises from Tilbury in the winter months.

Associated Humber Lines operated three Humber ferries for the British Transport Commission between Hull and New Holland. The *Lincoln Castle* (1940/598grt) was the only coal-fired paddle steamer in operation around the British Isles in her later years of service on the route.

Lincoln Castle, an Associated Humber Lines vessel (1940, 598grt, 64m x 10m, 13½ knots). She was sold in 1979 and became a restaurant/bar moored at Hessle. In 1988 she was relocated to Alexandra Dock at Grimsby.

Wingfield Castle also of Associated Humber Lines (1934, 556grt, 64m x 10m, 13½ knots). In 1974 she was sold and towed to London, and in 1977 was renamed *Brighton Belle*. In 1986 she was moved to Hartlepool.

CAMMELL LAIRD AND COMPANY (Shipbuilders & Engineers) LIMITED.

Launch of

M. V. "SPERO"

on

THURSDAY 5th. May 1966 at 11-50 a.m.

Admit ONE To SHIPYARD

GREEN LANE ENTRANCE ONLY

FOR CONDITIONS SEE BACK.

A launch ticket for Ellerman's Wilson Line *Spero*, and a sailing brochure for the 1969 season.

Associated Humber Lines' *Tattershall Castle* (1934, 556grt, 64m x 10m, 13 1/2 knots). She was sold in 1972 and towed to London in 1975. In 1991 she was overhauled at Rochester.

England of DFDS (1964, 8,221grt, 140m x 19m, 21 knots). She was sold to the Cunard Line in 1983 and was again resold and renamed *America XIII* in 1986, becoming *Emma* in 1988.

Three

Scotland

Services on the River Clyde were operated by the Caledonian Steam packet and David MacBrayne until their merger in 1973. They controlled a fleet of car ferries, paddle steamers and several smaller passenger vessels engaged in short sea crossings. Both companies provided a complex network of vehicle, passenger and excursion sailings on the Clyde and to the Western Islands.

The Stranraer to Larne service was managed by the Caledonian Steam Packer Company (Irish Services) Limited and was operated by the *Caledonian Princess* (1961/3629grt) and the *Antrim Princess* (1967/3630grt).

Burns and Laird Lines passenger and freight services linked Glasgow and Ardrossan with Belfast, with a nightly service in each direction on the Glasgow route supplemented by day sailings from Ardrossan.

A subsidiary of the Coast Lines Group, the North of Scotland Orkney and Shetland Shipping Company ran to Aberdeen, Leith to Kirkwall and Lerwick. The Orkney Isles Shipping Company provided the Thurso to Stromness inter-island passenger and cargo services.

Bute, a Caledonian Steam Packet vessel (1954, 570grt, 57m x 11m, 15½ knots). *Bute* became the *Med Sun* in 1980, but was laid up for four years and never sailed commercially under the Greek flag. She was broken up in Perama in 1984.

Cowal of the Caledonian Steam Packet (1954, 569 grt, 57m x 11m, 15½ knots). She suffered damage in a serious fire at Gourock in 1978 and was sold in 1979, becoming the *Mediterranean Star*. In 1983 she was broken up.

Caledonian Steam Packet vessel *Arran* (1953, 568grt, 57m x 11m, 15½ knots). In 1981 she was sold to Orisot Limited and towed to Dublin, then moved to Manchester in 1986 and renamed *Resolution*. In 1993 she was broken up at Manchester.

Queen Mary II of the Caledonian Steam Packet (1933, 871grt, 76m x 11m, 19 knots). She was built as the *Queen Mary* and given the suffix *II* in 1934. However, she became *Queen Mary* again in 1976 and in 1987 she was sold and moored at Waterloo Bridge on the River Thames.

Caledonia, another Caledonian Steam Packet vessel (1934, 623grt, 70m x 9m, 17 knots). In 1969 she was transferred to the ownership of the Scottish Transport Group and chartered to David MacBrayne. In 1970 she was renamed *Old Caledonia*. She was sold to Bass Charrington in 1972 and moored on the River Thames. On 27 April 1980 she was destroyed by fire and was broken up.

Caledonian Steam Packet vessel *Waverley* (1947, 396grt, 76m x 9m, 17 knots). She was transferred to the Scottish Transport Group in 1969 and in 1974 was operated by the Steamer Preservation Society. She is still in service, the last seagoing paddle steamer in the world.

David MacBrayne's *Lochfyne* (1931, 754grt, 67m x 9m, 15 knots). In 1973 she became the *Old Loch Fyne*, owned by Scottish & Newcastle Breweries Limited. She arrived at Dalmuir for breaking up on 25 March 1974.

St Ninian of North of Scotland, Orkney & Shetland Shipping (1950, 2,242grt, 87m x 14m, 15 knots). She was sold in 1976, renamed *Bucanero*, and was broken up at Guayaquil in 1991.

Countess of Breadalbane of the Caledonian Steam Packet (1936, 106grt, 28m x 5m, 10 knots). She was transferred to the Scottish Transport Group in 1969 and was renamed *Countess of Kempock* when she was purchased by W.R. Richie of Gourock in 1971. In 1979 she was sold to Offshore Workboats and was chartered to Staffa Marine. In 1982 she was taken inland to Loch Lomond where she became the *Countess Fiona* running with the *Maid of the Loch*. She was finally scrapped in 1999.

Earl of Zetland of North of Scotland,Orkney & Shetland Shipping (1939, 548grt, 51m x 9m, 12 knots). In 1976 she became the *Celtic Surveyor* and in 1982 was moored at Great Yarmouth as a floating restaurant. In 1996 she was moved to the River Tyne.

Maid of the Loch, a Caledonian Steam Packet vessel (1953, 555grt, 58m x 9m, 14 knots). In 1983 she was laid up at Balloch Pier and in 1992 was sold to Dumbarton Council. In 1994 she returned to service.

The Caledonian Steam Packet's *Maid of Cumbrae* (1953, 508grt, 49m x 9m, 15 knots). She was sold in 1978, becoming the *Hanseatic* and *Noce di Cocco*. In 1983 she was renamed *Capri Express*.

Maid of Argyll, also of the Caledonian Steam Packet (1953, 508grt, 49m x 9m, 15 knots). In 1974 she was sold to the Greeks and became the *City of Piraeus* and the *City of Corfu* in 1993. On 14 May 1997 she was destroyed by fire.

The Caledonian Steam Packet's *Caledonia*, (1966, 1,156grt, 62m x 12m, 19 knots). Built as the *Stena Baltica,* she was renamed *Caledonia* in 1970 and in 1990 became the *Heidi*.

King George V of David MacBrayne (1926, 791grt 80m x 10m, 20 knots). On 19 April 1975 she left Greenock in tow for Cardiff where she was laid up. On 25 August 1981 she suffered serious fire damage while being converted to a floating restaurant. She was broken up at Briton Ferry in 1982.

Glen Sannox of the Caledonian Steam Packet (1957, 1,107grt, 78m x 13m, 17½ knots). *Glen Sannox* became the *Knooz* in 1989, *Nadia* in 1990, *Al Marwah* in 1991 and *Al Basmalah I* in 1994.

Royal Ulsterman (1936, 3,290grt) and *Irish Coast* (1952, 3,824grt), berthed together at Glasgow.

Queen Mary II (1933, 871grt) and *Maid of Cumbrae* (1953, 508grt), on a busy summer weekend.

Loch Seaforth of David MacBrayne (1947, 1,090grt, 73m x 11m, 16 knots). She was built as the *Empire Maysong* and became *Loch Seaforth* in 1948. In 1973 she was sold to the West of Scotland Shipbreaking Company for demolition following grounding between Coll and Tiree. She was broken up in Troon later that year.

Two views of the *Royal Ulsterman* (1936, 3,290grt) which was renamed *Cammell Laird* in 1968 and *Sounion* in 1970. On 3 March 1973 she sank at Beirut following an underwater explosion and was refloated several weeks later on 17 April. She was broken up later that year.

Burns & Laird Scotland – Ireland motorway brochures featuring *Lion* and *Scottish coast*.

Lion (1967, 3,333grt) was built by Cammell Laird for Burns & Laird Lines for their Ardrossan -Belfast service. She became the Baroness M in 1985, Portelet in 1987 and Baroness M again in 1988. On 24 February 1990 she was attacked by a gunboat thirty miles off Jounieh on a voyage from Larnica. One passenger was killed.

Burns & Laid's *Royal Scotsman* (1936, 3,288grt, 104m x 15m, 17 knots). She became the *Apollo* in 1968 and was broken up in Brownsville, Texas in 1984.

Stena Nordica of Stena (1965, 2,607grt, 80m x 15m, 17 knots). *Stena Nordica* operated on the Stranraer to Larne route on charter to the Caledonian Steam Packet and was sold in 1973 to become the *Santa Ana*. On 7 May 1980 fire broke out in her engine room on a voyage between Puerto la Cruz and Punto de Piedras, Margarita Island. She was taken in tow, grounded and sank in shallow water.

Antrim Princess, owned by British Railways (1967, 3,270grt, 113m x 17m, 19½ knots). On 9 December 1983 she suffered an engine room fire and engine failure on a sailing from Larne to Stranraer in gale force winds. Passengers were lifted off by helicopter and the vessel was taken in tow to Harland &Wolff for repairs. These were completed on 28 December 1983. In 1985 she became the *Tynwald*, operating in Manx waters until 1990 when she was sold to Greek operators who renamed her *Lauro Express*.

Caledonian Princess of the Caledonian Steam Packet (1961, 3,629grt, 108m x 17m, 20½ knots). Sold to Quadrini Group in 1982, she was moored at Gateshead on the River Tyne in 1983 as the *Tuxedo Princess*. In 1988 she was moved to Glasgow and given the name *Caledonian Princess*. In 1998 she was moved back to the Tyne.

Four

Irish Sea

The main sea routes in the Irish Sea were those from England to Northern and Southern Ireland. These were operated by British Railways, the Belfast Steamship Company and the British & Irish Steam Packet Company.

British Railways operated the short sea routes between Holyhead and Dun Laoghaire, and Heysham to Belfast. The Belfast Steamship Company ran mainly night services between Liverpool and Belfast and these were supplemented by some day sailings in summer.

The British & Irish Steam Packet was originally a subsidiary of the Coast Lines Group and ownership was transferred to the Eire government in 1965. The line operated passenger and freight services between Dublin and Liverpool, and from Cork to Fishguard by the City of Cork Steam Packet.

The Isle of Man Steam Packet Company provided passenger services between Douglas and Liverpool, Fleetwood, Heysham, Belfast, Dublin and Ardrossan. They also operated a seasonal service between Liverpool and Llandudno when the Liverpool and North Wales Steamship Company went into voluntary liquidation in 1962.

Services between the Port of Preston and Northern Ireland were by the Transport Ferry Service Vessels *Ionic Ferry* (1958/2557grt) *Bardic Ferry* (1957/2550grt) and the *Empire Nordic* (1945/4157grt) chartered from the Ministry of Transport.

On the River Mersey the Birkenhead Corporation ran the service from Woodside to Liverpool, and the Seacombe to Liverpool Pier Head was the responsibility of the Wallasey Corporation, with the *Royal Iris* (1951/1234grt) offering dance and Mersey river cruises.

Lady of Mann (1930, 3,104grt) passes *Ben my Chree* (1966, 2,762grt) in Douglas Harbour in 1968.

Isle of Man Steam Packet vessels berthed at Victoria Pier, Douglas.

Monas Isle (1951, 2,491grt) prepares to sail to Liverpool as *Tynwald* (1947, 2,487grt) arrives on a special excursion from Fleetwood.

A quiet Sunday morning at Princes Landing Stage at Liverpool in July 1967. *King Orry* (1946, 2,485grt) loads passengers for a sailing to Llandudno. *Lady of Mann* and *Tynwald* rest at the north end of the stage.

Ben my Chree of the Isle of Man Steam Packet (1927, 2,586grt, 112m x 14m, 22 knots). She was broken up in 1966.

Another *Ben my Chree* of the Isle of Man Steam Packet (1966, 2,762grt, 105m x 16m, 21 knots). The *Ben* was sold in 1985 and was chartered back to the Steam Packet for the busy Tourist Trophy period in June of that year. She was broken up in Santander, Spain, in 1989 after being laid up in Vittoria Dock, Birkenhead.

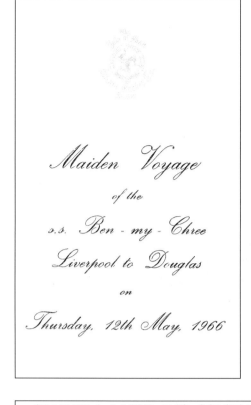

Maiden Voyage

of the

s.s. Ben - my - Chree

Liverpool to Douglas

on

Thursday, 12th May, 1966

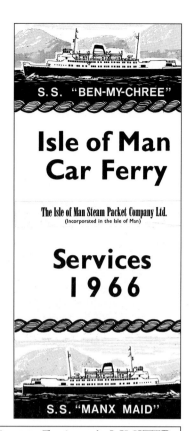

S.S. "BEN-MY-CHREE"

Isle of Man Car Ferry

The Isle of Man Steam Packet Company Ltd.
(Incorporated in the Isle of Man)

Services 1966

S.S. "MANX MAID"

CAMMELL LAIRD AND COMPANY (Shipbuilders & Engineers) LIMITED

Launch of

T S. S. "BEN-MY-CHREE"

on

FRIDAY 10th December 1965 at 11-30 a.m.

ADMIT ONE TO SHIPYARD

GREEN LANE ENTRANCE ONLY

FOR CONDITIONS SEE BACK.

Launch ticket, maiden voyage menu and car ferry brochure for *Ben my Chree*.

The Isle of Man Steam Packet's *Manxman* (1955, 2,495grt, 105m x 15m, 21 knots). She was sold to new owners in 1982 and berthed at the Port of Preston. In 1990 she was moved to Liverpool and in 1994 berthed at Hull. In 1997 she was towed to Sunderland where she sank at her berth in 1999.

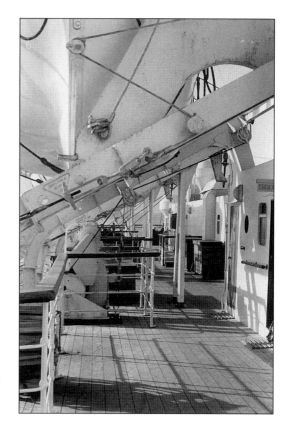

Above and right: Manx Maid of the Isle of Man Steam Packet (1962, 2,724grt, 105m x 16m, 21 knots). In 1985 she was sold and towed to Bristol. However, it was not possible to obtain planning permission for her static role and she was broken up at Garston in 1986.

OLD PEOPLE'S HOLIDAYS

24th May to 7th June   14th June to 28th June
and 6th September to 20th September

INTERNATIONAL CYCLING WEEK FESTIVAL
14th June to 21st June

Full particulars from Secretary, Tourist Board, Douglas.

ANNUAL INTERNATIONAL DANCE FESTIVAL WEEK (OLD TIME) AT DOUGLAS
23rd August to 30th August

Brochure from Festival Secretary, Town Hall, Douglas.

PASSENGER FARES	Single	Return
DOUGLAS, LIVERPOOL, HEYSHAM, BELFAST and DUBLIN .... }	47/6	80/-
ARDROSSAN	55/-	85/-
LLANDUDNO	35/-	62/6

Mid-week tickets between Liverpool, Heysham and Douglas
70/- Return

OUTWARD
On Tuesday, Wednesday, or Thursday.

RETURN
On either Tuesday, Wednesday or Thursday within a period of three months.

Children under three years of age FREE; three years and under 14 years, HALF-FARE. Infants must be accompanied by an adult.

All fares are current at time of publication and are liable to alteration without notice.

Passengers and their accompanied luggage will only be carried subject to the Company's Standard Conditions of Carriage of Passengers and Passengers' Accompanied Property as exhibited in the Company's Offices and on board its vessels. Acceptance of a ticket issued by the Company binds the passenger to these conditions.

CATERING

Breakfasts, Luncheons, High Teas and Suppers are available at reasonable charges. Buffets available for light refreshments.

All steamers are fully licensed and carry a wide assortment of Ales, Wines, Spirits, Minerals, Cigarettes and Confectionery.

GENERAL INFORMATION

PASSENGER TICKETS can be purchased in advance. TRANSPORT AT RAILWAY STATIONS — from 23rd May to 13th September inclusive, passengers travelling by main line trains connecting with the steamers from Liverpool will be conveyed by special Corporation buses from Lime Street and Exchange Stations, Liverpool, to Princes Parade, adjoining the steamer at a nominal charge. Passengers travelling from Douglas between 23rd May and 30th September inclusive, will be conveyed to the Stations named at a similar charge.

All the accommodation in the Saloons is free and cannot be reserved.

Passage times shown are approximate being subject to weather and tidal conditions.

The Isle of Man Steam Packet Company Ltd.
(Incorporated in the Isle of Man)

ISLE OF MAN
PASSENGER SERVICES
1st MAY–30th SEPTEMBER
1969

The Company may alter, withdraw, or curtail any service, or suspend or cancel any sailing as the Company may think necessary

TICKETS OBTAINABLE AS UNDER :—

ARDROSSAN–McBride's Shipping Agencies Ltd., 93 Hope St., Glasgow, C.2. Telephone: Glasgow 041 248 5161.

BELFAST—W. E. Williames & Co. Ltd., 82/86 High St. Telephone: Belfast 0232 29281. Telex 74619.

DUBLIN—British & Irish Steam Packet Co. Ltd., 16 Westmoreland Street. Telephone: Dublin 777345.

HEYSHAM—Capt. Blackmore, Shipping & Port Manager. Telephone: Heysham 0524 52373.

LIVERPOOL—Thomas Orford & Son, India Buildings, 40 Brunswick Street. Telephone: Liverpool 051 236 3214. Telex 62415

LLANDUDNO—Mr. S. Bouwman, Pier Booking Office (Summer Only). Telephone: Llandudno 76837.

MORECAMBE—Visitor Travel Agency, Victoria Street. Telephone: Morecambe 4531.

Also at principal Main Line Stations of British Railways; Booking Offices of Thos. Cook & Son, Ltd.; Co-operative Travel Service; Frames' Tours Ltd.; Lewis's Ltd.; and all other principal Travel Agents.

THE ISLE OF MAN STEAM PACKET CO. LTD.
P.O. Box 5, Imperial Buildings, Douglas, Isle of Man.
Telephone: Douglas 0624 3824. Telex 62414
RAMSEY OFFICE, Telephone: Ramsey 0624 81 2110.

S. R. SHIMMIN,
December, 1968.   General Manager.

THE NORRIS MODERN PRESS LTD., DOUGLAS, I.O.M.

Isle of Man Steam Packet timetable for their passenger services in 1969.

Tynwald of the Isle of Man Steam Packet (1947, 2,487grt, 105m x 14m, 21 knots). She was sold in 1974 and left the River Mersey on 3 February 1975 for the shipbreakers at Newport, Gwent. She was resold by Cashmore to Spanish shipbreakers and arrived in tow at Aviles on 10 February 1975. Her whistle was transferred and fitted to the *Ben my Chree*.

Monas Isle of The Isle of Man Steam Packet (1951, 2,491grt, 105m x 14m, 21 knots). She left Birkenhead for Ouwerkerk on 28 October 1980 for breaking up.

The Isle of Man Steam Packet's *King Orry* (1946, 2,485grt, 105m x 14m, 21 knots). She was sold in 1975 and went aground at Glasson Dock. She was eventually broken up in 1979.

Car deck on the *Manx Maid* (1962, 2,724grt) on a light sailing from Douglas to Liverpool.

Norwest Laird of Norwest Shipping (1939, 577grt, 58m x 10m, 13 knots). She was built as the *Lochiel* for service in Scotland and was bought by Norwest for a new service to the Isle of Man in 1970. However, as she proved to be unsuitable for this route, she was sold to Courage (Weston) Ltd in 1974 and berthed at Hayle in Cornwall, where this photograph was taken. In 1978 she was moved to Bristol, renamed *Lochiel*, and survived until 1996 when she was broken up.

Stella Marina (1965, 1,339grt) leaving Douglas, Isle of Man for Fleetwood. She was chartered to Norwest Shipping Ltd.

Following page: *Snaefell* (1948, 2,489grt) berthed in the East Float, Birkenhead. She was sold to Blyth Shipbreakers and left the Mersey on 23 August 1978 in tow to be broken up.

Manxman (1955, 2,495grt) was the first steamer to arrive at the Isle of Man on 2 July 1966 following the six week national Seaman's strike.

Morpeth Dock, Birkenhead was the regular winter lay up berth for the Isle of Man boats in the 1960s.

Lady of Mann of the Isle of Man Steam Packet (1930, 3,104grt, 113m x 15m, 22 knots). The flagship of the fleet was broken up in 1971.

Isle of Man 'contractors' socialize on the ramp of the *Manx Maid* on a sailing to Douglas in 1965.

Motorcycles are unloaded from the *Snaefell* at Douglas at the begining of the Tourist Trophy week in June 1962.

Some passengers relax and enjoy the sea air on the promenade deck of *Ben my Chree* (1927, 2,586grt) on a sailing from Belfast to Douglas.

Passenger deck on *Ben my Chree* (1966, 2,762grt).

Ulster Monarch of the Belfast Steamship Company (1929, 3,735grt, 109m x 14m, 17 knots). She was broken up at Ghent in 1967.

The Belfast Steamship Company's *Ulster Prince* (1937, 4,303grt, 112m x 15m, 17 knots). Built as the *Leinster* for the Liverpool to Dublin service of the B+I, she became the *Ulster Prince I* in 1966. She was renamed *Adria* in 1968 for service in Greece, and became *Odysseus* in 1969. She returned home and was laid up at Glasgow from 22 July 1977, before being broken up at Faslane when she arrived there on 2 October 1979.

Irish Coast of Coast Lines (1952, 3,824grt, 104m x 16m, 17½ knots). Following completion of her service for Coast Lines she was laid up in Morpeth Dock at Birkenhead and sold to the Greeks in 1968, being renamed *Orpheus*. In 1969 she was renamed *Semiramis II*, *Achilleus*, and *Apollon II* and in 1981 became the *Regency*. She was broken up in Manila in 1989.

Ulster Monarch, Ulster Prince, Tynwald and *Snaefell* laid up in Morpeth Dock, Birkenhead in 1966.

Innisfallen of B+I Line (1948, 3,705grt, 104m x 15m, 17 knots). She was renamed *Innisfallen I* and *Poseidonia* in 1969 and sailed in Greek waters until she was broken up at Brindisi in 1985.

B+I Line's *Munster* (1948, 4,088grt, 112m x 15m, 17½ knots). She was renamed *Munster I*, *Theseus* and *Orpheus* in 1969.

Leinster (1948, 4,115grt, 112m x 15m, 17½ knots) and *Ulster Prince* (1967, 4,479grt) loading in Princes Dock, Liverpool.

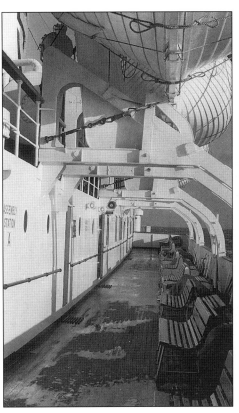

A rare daylight sailing on *Munster* (1948, 4,088grt) from Dublin to Liverpool.

Leinster was bought by Greek owners in 1969 and renamed *Leinster I* and *Aphrodite*. She operated short cruises until she was broken up at Aliga, where she arrived on 11 October 1987.

CAMMELL LAIRD AND COMPANY (Shipbuilders & Engineers) LIMITED.

Launch of

M. V. "ULSTER QUEEN"

on

THURSDAY 1st December 1966 at 12-15 p.m.

ADMIT ONE TO SHIPYARD

GREEN LANE ENTRANCE ONLY

FOR CONDITIONS SEE BACK.

Above and next page: Official launch ticket for *Ulster Queen* at Cammell Laird Shipyard on 1 December 1966. Ticket for special excursion on *St Clair* (1960, 3,303grt). She sailed from Aberdeen at 13.00 on 8 February 1970, passed Rathlin Head at 17.20 on 9 February and the Calf of Man at 23.35 the same day. On 10 February she passed the Bar Lightship at 04.35, anchored in the river at 06.00 and docked at Princes Dock at 11.45.

71.

14

BELFAST STEAMSHIP CO. LTD.

SPECIAL EXCURSION TICKET

M.V. ST. CLAIR

ABERDEEN to LIVERPOOL

Depart Aberdeen SUNDAY, 8th FEBRUARY, 1970

FARE (including use of Berth) - £7 0s 0d

CONDITIONS OF CARRIAGE

Passengers, vehicles and luggage are only carried subject to the Company's Standard Conditions of Carriage as exhibited in the Company's offices and on board their ships. All sailings are subject to alteration or cancellation without prior notice. Fares and rates subject to revision.

Ulster Prince of the Belfast Steamship Company (1967, 4,479grt, 115m x 17m, 17 knots). She became the *Lady* M in 1982, *Tangpakorn* in 1984, *Longhu* and *Macmosa* in 1988, *Neptunia* in 1994 and *Panther* in 1996.

Ulster Queen, also of the Belfast Steamship Company (1967, 4,479grt, 115m x 17m, 17 knots). She was sold to Greek owners in 1982 and became *Med Sea*. In 1986 she was renamed *Al Kahera* and *Ala-Eddin* in 1987 and *Poseidonia* in 1988.

A band serenades passengers at Dublin as *Leinster* (1968, 4,848grt) moves astern into the River Liffey at the start of her maiden voyage to Liverpool.

Irish Coast, Ulster Monarch, Kilkenny, Meath and *Munster* in Princes Dock, Liverpool.

Leinster of B+I Line (1968, 4,848grt, 118m x 18m, 21 knots). In 1980 she was transferred to the Southern Irish Sea route and renamed *Innisfallen*. In 1986 she was sold and renamed *Chams* and *Ionian Sun*. In 1990 she became the *Celtic Pride II* and the *Ionian Sun* again in 1991.

Munster of the B+I Line (1968, 4,230grt, 110m x 18m, 21 knots). Sold in 1983, she was renamed *Farah, Farah I* in 1984 and *Tian Peng* in 1991.

1968-1969 B+I LINE

EXCURSIONS

LIVERPOOL
to DUBLIN

BY THE NEW CAR FERRY
m/v "MUNSTER"

ONE CLASS **59/-** RETURN

19th NOVEMBER 1968 to 17th MAY 1969
(Except during the period
19th December 1968 to 1st January 1969. Also 3rd April 1969)

DAY
DEPART LIVERPOOL (CARRIERS DOCK)
every TUESDAY and THURSDAY
Return from DUBLIN (FERRYPORT) the following day

WEEK-END
DEPART LIVERPOOL (CARRIERS DOCK)
every SATURDAY
Return from DUBLIN (FERRYPORT) the following Monday

Embarkation at both ports from 20-00 hours

Vessel sails at 22-15 hours

Apply — B+I LINE
COAST LINES LIMITED (Agents)

Reliance House, Water Street, Liverpool
L2 8TS
Telephone : 051-236 5464

Robert McGee & Co. Ltd., 19 Old Hall Street, Liverpool, 3.

B+I Line 1968-1969 leaflet for day and weekend excursions on the *Munster* from Liverpool to Dublin.

Innisfallen of B+I Line (1968, 4,849grt, 118m x 18m, 21 knots). She became the *Corsica Viva* in 1980, *Dominican Viva* in 1985, *Corsica Viva I* in 1988, *Sardinia Viva* and *Cariba Viva* in 1993, *Spirit of Independence* in 1994 and *Happy Dolphin* in 1999.

Passenger and cargo vessels loading in the River Liffey. *Munster* (1948, 4,088grt) prepares to sail to Liverpool and *Tynwald* (1947, 2,487grt) to Douglas.

British Railway's *Holyhead Ferry I* (1965, 3,879grt, 112m x 17m, 19½ knots). Renamed *Earl Leofric* in 1976, she was broken up at San Esteban de Pravia who commenced work on 29 June 1981.

Cambria of British Railways (1949, 5,284grt, 121m x 16m, 21 knots). She became the *Altaif* in 1976, and sank in 1980.

Hampton Ferry of British Railways (1934, 2,989grt, 106m x 19m, 16½ knots). She was photographed in 1971 laid up at Holyhead, North Wales, when she was sold and renamed *Tre Arddur*. She was broken up at Valencia in 1973.

A British Railways vessel, *Hibernia* (1949, 4,972grt, 121m x 16 m, 21 knots). Sold in 1976 and renamed *Express Apollon*, she arrived at Piraeus on 15 December that year. She was laid up for four years and was sold to breakers at Bombay where she arrived on 18 December 1980.

Holyhead Ferry I passes *Hibernia* in Dun Laoghaire Harbour on a sailing to Holyhead.

The British United hovercraft that operated the world's first hovercraft service from Leasowe, Wirral, to Rhyl in North Wales This photograph shows her leaving Alfred Dock, Birkenhead, for trials in the Irish Sea prior to starting the service on 20 July 1962.

St Tudno of the Liverpool & North Wales Steamship Company (1926, 2,326grt, 97m x 13m, $20\frac{1}{2}$knots). When her owners ceased trading and went into voluntary liquidation in 1963 she was sold to shipbreakers in Ghent.

An Isle of Man steamer arrives at Llandudno, North Wales on a day excursion from Liverpool.

PARTY OUTINGS

by SEA to

NORTH WALES

View of Llandudno from the sea

TIME TABLE — 1962 SEASON

T.S. "ST. TUDNO"

**DAILY from Saturday, 9th June to Sunday, 16th September
(except Fridays during June, July and September)**

OUTWARD		HOMEWARD	
Liverpool	dep. 10.45 a.m.	**Menai Bridge**	dep. 3.45 p.m.
To **Llandudno**	due 1.05 p.m.	To **Llandudno**	due 5.00 p.m.
	dep. 1.15 p.m.		dep. 5.15 p.m.
To **Menai Bridge** due	2.40 p.m.	To **Liverpool**	due 7.40 p.m.

BUFFET LUNCHES AND TEAS

May be obtained in the Dining Saloons of "St. Tudno"

Light Refreshments are available in the Cafeteria and Buffets on board.

★ ★ ★

Arrangements can be made with Catering establishments in Llandudno for parties requiring Lunch. Menus can be submitted on application to the Secretary of the Company.

ALL VESSELS FULLY LICENSED

SEE INSIDE FOR REDUCED FARES FOR ORGANISED PARTY EXCURSIONS . . . .

Liverpool & North Wales Steamship 'Party Outings' leaflet and timetable for the 1962 season sailings from Liverpool to Llandudno and Menai Bridge.

St Trillo (1936, 314grt) sails around Puffin Island off Angelsey on an afternoon cruise from Llandudno.

Monas Isle (1951, 2,491grt) berths at Llandudno Pier as *King Orry* (1946, 2,485grt) sails to Liverpool.

WHITE FUNNEL FLEET

Sailings from

LIVERPOOL

(Princes Landing Stage)

by the Motor Vessel "QUEEN OF THE ISLES"

The Queen of the Isles is a vessel of 515 tons, is licensed by the Board of Trade to carry 300 passengers anywhere in the United Kingdom. The vessel has ample covered accommodation, and delightful open decks. Light refreshment can be obtained and the fully licensed bar remains open throughout the voyage.

Saturdays July 27th & August 10th & 31st

Grand Afternoon Cruise along the Coast, passing the Bar Lightship and across Liverpool Bay towards Blackpool.

Leave Liverpool at 3.15 p.m. back 5.0 p.m.

Fare 8/6d. Children 3—14 Half Price.

Single trip to Llandudno and Menai Bridge.

Leave Liverpool 5.15 p.m. due Llandudno 8.0 p.m. Menai Bridge 9.30 p.m.

Fares Llandudno 22/6 Menai Bridge 25/- (Children 3—14 half price).

Note: The Queen of the Isles leaves Menai Bridge 10.20 a.m. Llandudno 12 noon for Liverpool (due 2.45 p.m.).

FOR GENERAL INFORMATION, AND CONDITIONS OF CARRIAGE—PLEASE SEE OVERLEAF

The White Funnel Line chartered the *Queen of the Isles* (1965, 515grt) for a number of sailings in the Irish Sea in 1968.

St Trillo of the Liverpool & North Wales Steamship Company (1936, 314grt, 48m x 8m, 13½ knots). She was built as the *St Sirio* and became the *St Trillo* in 1945. She was sold to Townsend Brothers Limited in 1963 and converted to a floating restaurant in 1972. In 1975 she was broken up at Dublin.

Queen of the Isles of the Isles of Scilly Steamship Company (1965, 515grt, 48m x 9m, 13 knots). In 1971 she became *Olovaha*, *Gulf Explorer* in 1982, *Queen of the Isles* in 1987, *Island Princess* in 1994 and *Western Queen* in 1994. She was beached at Ranadi following Cyclone Justin in 1997.

Balmoral of P & A Campbell (1949, 736grt, 62m x 10m, 15 knots). Sold to P&A Campbell in 1981 and resold to Craig Inns, Dundee in 1982. In 1986 she was bought by Helseam Limited and in 1995 was sold to the Waverley Steam Navigation Company.

St Trillo berthed at Menai Bridge Pier in 1961.

Mountwood of Mersey Ferries (1960, 464grt, 46m x 12m, 12 knots). A member of the present Mersey ferry fleet.

Mersey Ferries' *Overchurch* (1962, 468grt, 47m x 12m, 12 knots). In 1999 she was partly rebuilt for cruise work and renamed *Royal Daffodil*.

Woodchurch of Mersey Ferries (1960, 464grt, 46m x 12m, 12 knots). She is still in service on the Mersey.

A Wallasey Corporation vessel, *Royal Daffodil II* (1958, 609grt, 48m x 15m, 12 knots). She was built as the *Royal Daffodil II* and was renamed in 1968. She completed her service on the Mersey in 1978 and was sold to Greek owners who renamed her *Ioulis Keas II*. She became the *Agia Kyriaki* in 1990.

Leasowe, another Wallasey Corporation ship (1951, 567grt, 45m x 10m, 12 knots). She was renamed *Naias II* in 1974 and *Cavo Doro* in 1980.

Egremont of the Wallasey Corporation (1952, 566grt, 45m x 10m, 12 knots). She was sold to the Island Cruising Club, Salcombe, Devon in 1976.

The Wallasey Corporation's *Royal Iris* (1951, 1,234grt, 48m x 15m, 12 knots). In 1994 she was sold as a restaurant ship berthed at Liverpool. She was moved to Cardiff in 1995 and to London in 1998.

Birkenhead and Wallasey Corporation ferries berth at the landing stage at Liverpool while the *Manx Maid* (1962, 2,724grt) loads passengers and cars for a sailing to Douglas, Isle of Man.

Duke of Argyll of British Railways (1956, 4,450grt, 115m x 17m, 21 knots). She operated the last Heysham to Belfast sailing on 5 April 1975, returning light on 9 April. She was sold later in 1975 and renamed *Neptunia*, before becoming *Corinthia* in 1988, *Faith Power* in 1993, *Fairy Princess* in 1994 and *Zenith* in 1995. She was broken up in China in 1996.

Duke of Lancaster (1956, 4,797grt) docks at her berth at Belfast as *Lion* (1967, 3,333grt) prepares to sail to Ardrossan.

Duke of Rothesay of British Railways (1956, 4,780grt, 115m x 17m, 21 knots). She operated the final Belfast-Heysham sailing on 5 April 1975. She arrived at Faslane for breaking up on 18 October 1975.

British Railways' *Duke of Lancaster* (1956, 4,797grt, 115m x 17m, 21 knots). She was moored on the River Dee in North Wales as a leisure attraction as the *Duke of Llanerch-y-mor* in 1980.

Bardic Ferry of the Atlantic Steam Navigation (1957, 2,550grt, 103m x 16m, 14 knots). She was sold in 1976, became the *Nasim II,* and was broken up at Aliga where she arrived on 5 November 1988.

Lion (1967, 3,333grt) prepares to sail from Belfast with the *Duke of Lancaster* (1956, 4,797grt) berthed astern.

Ionic Ferry of the Atlantic Steam Navigation (1958, 2,557grt, 103m x 17m, 14 knots). She was renamed *Kamasin* in 1976 and *Tamerlane* in 1980. On 9 April 1988 she arrived at Aliga for breaking up.

Five
Coastal Cargo Vessels

An active coastal shipping trade developed in the 1950s and 1960s. Several companies owned large fleets which traded within the United Kingdom and further afield, to European ports.

Coast Lines, who operated passenger as well as cargo ships, were the parent company for a number of smaller shipping lines which traded around the coast. By 1966 F.T. Everard owned seventy-five ships trading in general cargo and oil and the General Steam Navigation Company of London owned thirty-four coastal vessels. Esso and Shell-Mex and BP each had large fleets of coastal tankers.

The islands around the coast of the British Isles were served by small fleets of cargo vessels. David MacBrayne, North of Scotland, the Orkney & Shetland Shipping Company and the Ramsay Steamship Company each provided vital shipping services to their respective communities.

Some large firms owned their own coastal vessels. Imperial Chemical Industries (ICI) operated vessels for their Mond and Nobel Divisions, the North Thames Gas Board owned two ships and Arthur Guinness shipped their product from Dublin to Liverpool by specialist vessels.

John Summers & Sons' *Staley Bridge* (1940, 297grt, 42m x 8m, 9 knots). She was broken up at Bow Creek in 1991.

Ben Maye of the Ramsey Steamship Company (1921, 323grt, 40m x 7m, 10 knots). Built as the *Tod Head*, she was renamed *Kyle Rhea* in 1931 and *Ben Maye* in 1955. Broken up at Troon in 1964.

Centricity of F.T. Everard (1955, 655 grt, 56m x 9m, 10 knots). She was sold in 1977 and became *Demi* and *Magdalena* in 1979. She was broken up at Vianen, Holland in 1982.

Race Fisher (1942, 739grt) was a member of the James Fisher fleet.

Lairdsglen of Burns & Laird Lines (1954, 1,543grt, 91m x 13m, 14 knots). She was converted to a livestock carrier in 1969 and renamed *Devon Express* in 1974. She was broken up at Cartagena in 1983.

Darlington of Associated Humber Lines (1958, 963grt, 71m x 12m, 12½knots). She was renamed *Gulf Sky* in 1971, *Abadan* in 1977 and *Petros P* and *Ekaterini P* in 1978. She was abandoned at Brest in 1980, then towed to sea and sunk in 1982.

Vacuum Pioneer of the Vacuum Oil Company (1953, 1,650grt, 79m x 12m, 11 knots). She collided with *Worthing* (1957, 1,873grt) off Haisborough on 13 October 1970. She arrived at Hughes Bolckow at Blyth for demolition on 24 October 1970.

Ben Bates of Shell Mex & BP (1956, 565grt, 55m x 9m, 10 knots). In 1973 she was sold to Woodwards Oil, Goose Bay, Labrador and was renamed *Tana Woodward*.

Egret (1959, 1,187grt) operated for the British & Continental Steamship Company on services to Amsterdam, Rotterdam and Dunkirk.

Aberthaw Fisher of James Fisher & Sons (1966, 2,355grt, 84m x 16m, 12 knots). She was renamed *National Generation* in 1990, *Aberthaw Fisher* in 1992 and *Moonstar* in 1996.

Ballyhill of John Kelly (1954, 986grt, 70m x 10m, 10 knots). She left Falmouth in tow on 25 September 1973 for Gijon, Spain, where she was broken up.

John Kelly's *Ballyrush* (1962, 1,575grt, 78m x 12m, 11½ knots). In 1985 she became the *Otterburn*, *Stina Star* in 1986, *Polly C* in 1988, *Polly Anna* in 1989, *Med Prince* and *Karim* in 1992 and the *Haidar 3* in 1995.

Glanmire of the City of Cork Steam Packet (1936, 695grt, 72m x 11m, 12 knots). Built as the *Lairdsbank*, she became the *Glanmire* in 1963 and was broken up at Dalmuir in 1969.

Cheshire Coast of Coast Lines (1954, 1,202grt, 78m x 12m, 12 knots). She was renamed *Malabar* and *Spartan Prince* in 1967, *Cheshire Coast* and *Venture* in 1971 and *Azelia* in 1974. She was broken up in 1980.

COASTAL CRUISES

Belfast

Dublin

Liverpool

Cork

London

Southampton

Plymouth

is year, for a holiday that's really different, take a coastal cruise - a mini
a-cruise around the fascinating coast of Britain with a call at Dublin or
rk and opportunities for sightseeing.

Coast Line coastal cruise offers you all the mental and physical benefits
a sea cruise in the friendly and informal atmosphere of a cargo liner.

e service is operated by "Hibernian Coast" and "Caledonian Coast"
ween London and Liverpool, providing amidships accommodation for a
ited number of passengers.

gle and double cabins are available and there is a friendly dining room,
nge and bar for passengers' comfort.

th motor vessels are equipped with radio telephone, radar and other
vigational aids.

come coastal cruising this year - but to avoid disappointment please make
ur booking **now**. Passenger accommodation on each ship is limited to
persons.

m.v. Caledonian Coast
m.v. Hibernian Coast

DEPART LIVERPOOL

Weekly every Friday/Saturday 14th/15th April to 15th/16th
September, inclusive.
Embark: Friday 16.30 hours.

*Ports of call (if any) between Liverpool and London according to
cargo requirements.*
London arrive Wednesday, a.m.

DEPART LONDON

Every Friday from Friday 21st April to Friday 22nd September,
inclusive.
Embark: 18.30 hours.
Dublin arrive Sunday p.m.; sail Tuesday p.m.
Liverpool arrive Wednesday, a.m.

Coast Lines brochure detailing coastal cruises between Liverpool and London, calling at a
number of other British and Irish ports.

Tay of Burns & Laird Lines (1951, 782grt, 71m x 11m, 12 knots). Built as the *Western Coast*, she was renamed *Tay* in 1958. She became *Charalambos* in 1968 and *Erika* in 1973. She sank in 1973.

Talisker of Burns & Laird Lines (1955, 1,016grt, 75m x 12m, 11 knots). Built as the *Ulster Pioneer*, she became *Talisker* in 1963, *Bat Snapir* in 1970, *Woodbine* in 1973 and *Hong Shen* in 1975. She sank in 1988.

Above: Ikaria (1949, 995grt) on a
nostalgic return to Liverpool in 1970.
She was originally built as the *Lairds Ben*
for Burns & Laird Lines, and became the
Brookmount in 1959. Sold in 1970, she
was renamed *Ikaria*, and *Pierre Rodolphe*
in 1971, *Ziad* in 1973 and *Sweet Waves*
in 1979. She sank at Tripoli in 1983.

Right: Colebrooke of the Belfast
Steamship Company (1948, 990grt, 87m
x 12m, 11 knots). Built as the *Lairsmoor*,
she became *Colebrooke* in 1960. In 1970
she was renamed *Mirna* and in 1984 she
sank off Yugoslavia.

Bison of Link Line (1961, 2,144grt, 79m x 13m, 12 knots). In 1972 she was transferred to North Sea Ferries and renamed *Norbank*. She was sold in 1979 when she was renamed *Flamingo*. She continued in service until 1997 when she was laid up.

The Belfast Steamship Company's *Mountstewart* (1955, 892grt, 69m x 11m, 11 knots). She was built as the *Essex Coast* and became the *Mountstewart* in 1957, *Evdelos* in 1969, *Michalis* in 1972, *Proodos* in 1976 and *Manuel* in 1979. She was broken up in 1986.

Wicklow of the B+I Line (1938, 586grt, 60m x 10m, 11 knots). Built as the *Sandhill*, in 1946 she became the *Valerian Coast*, then *Hebridean Coast* in 1948, *Ulster Chieftain* in 1953, *Durham Coast* in 1956 and the *Wicklow* in 1960. In 1970 she was renamed *Sinergasia*, then *Sonia* in 1973 and *Margarita P* in 1974. She was finally broken up in 1980.

Kilkenny, also of the B+I Line (1937, 1,320grt, 84m x 12m, 12 knots). In 1971 she was sold and renamed *Cork*. On 27 May 1974 her engines failed off Holyhead and she was towed to Dublin. As it was uneconomical to repair her she was sold to the shipbreakers.

Bitola (1947, 1,655grt) was built as *Adria*. She became the *Bitola* in 1963, *Taras* in 1968 and *Indian Ocean* in 1971. In 1973 she was renamed *Dimitris K* owned by Triakapa Shipping, Panama. On 20 December 1979 she sank on a voyage from Venice to Massawa.

Valzell of J. Tyrell (1935, 576grt, 54m x 9m, $9\frac{1}{2}$ knots). Built as the *Arbroath* she became *Valzell* in 1963 and was broken up at Cork in 1972.

The Lady Patricia, an Arthur Guinness vessel (1963, 1,187grt, 65m x 12m, 11 knots). She was sold in 1993 and renamed *Maine*.

The Lady Gwendolen, also of Arthur Guinness (1953, 1,164grt, 65m x 11m, 11 knots). Sold in 1977, she was renamed *Paros*. She sank off Ravenna Roads in 1979.

Ben Veg of the Ramsey Steamship Company (1965, 346grt, 44m x 8m, 8 knots). She was sold to the Tyne Shiprepair Group in 1979 and then to Brigham & Cowan Limited. She was sold to the Interisland Shipping Company of Grenada in 1980 and ,on 4 August that year, she went aground off Bridgetown, Bahamas during hurricane 'Allen'. She was refloated on 9 August and was later renamed *The Benn*. Her name was altered to *Benn* in 1985. On 17 January 1991 she was being towed from Port of Spain to Castries when she sank at 11.20N, 65.00W.

Ben Vooar (1950, 427grt) was owned by the Ramsey Steamship Company. She was sold in 1976 and renamed *Arran Firth* and in 1982 was purchased by the St Ives Motor & Marine Company of Panama.

Glengariff (1936, 1,599grt) was built as the *Rathlin* and was bought by Burns & Laird Lines in 1953 and renamed *Lairdscraig*. She became *Glengariff* in 1956 and was broken up in 1964.

Ben Rein of the Ramsey Steamship Company (1947, 393grt, 45m x 8m, 10 knots). Built as *Lita*, she was renamed *Tamara* in 1954 and *Ben Rein* in 1956.

Ramsey of the Isle of Man Steam Packet (1965, 446grt, 45m x 9m, 12 knots). Sold by the Steam Packet in 1974, she was renamed *Hoofort*, She became the *Boa Entrado* in 1982 and the *Arquipelago* in 1990.

Christopher Rowbotham's *Helmsman* (1937, 493grt) passes the breakwater at Douglas, Isle of Man, in June 1962.

Fenella of the Isle of Man Steam Packet (1951, 1,019grt, 64m x11m, 12 knots). Sold in 1973 and renamed *Vasso M*, she caught fire and sank in February 1977.

Peveril, also of the Isle of Man Steam Packet (1964, 1,048grt, 63m x 12m, 12 knots). She became the *Nadalena H* in 1981, *Virginia Luck* in 1982, *Akak Princess* in 1983, *Zeina* in 1984, *Akak Star* in 1986, *Mariana I* and *MJKV* in 1991, *Ayah* in 1999 and *Mihmandar* in 2000.

Conister of the Isle of Man Steam Packet (1932, 411grt, 44m x 7m, 10 knots). Built as *Abington*, she was broken up at Dalmuir in 1965.

Isle of Man Steam Packet vessel *Peveril* (1929, 798grt, 65m x 11m, 12 knots). She was broken up at Glasson Dock in 1964.

Adrian M of Metcalfe Motor Coasters (1957, 967grt, 66m x 10m, 11 knots). She became the *Hero* in 1970, *Burnley* in 1972 and was broken up at Manchester in 1983.

G.T. Gillie & Blair's vessel *Moray Firth IV* (1960, 613grt).

Finnwood of Finnlines (1956, 1,185grt, 84m x 12m, 12 knots). Built as the *Ebbella*, she became the *Orizaba* in 1956, *Finnwood* in 1959, *Rex* in 1970, *Mar del Nord* in 1974 and *Sri Lanka* in 1983. She was broken up at Ortona in 1984.

Loris (1943, 2,850grt) was owned by Cia Nav Le and was built as the *Empire Jessica*. In 1945 she was renamed *Joseph Blot* and *Leon Mazzella*, before becoming *Loris* in 1954.

Varodd of Egil Naesheim AS (1958, 1,921grt, 82m x 12m, 10 knots). She was renamed *Estremadurian* in 1968 and reverted to *Varodd* again in 1970. In 1975 she became *Petrola XL* and *Petrola 40* and was broken up in 1995.

Farringay (1944, 461grt) owned by J.H. Griffin of Great Yarmouth arriving at Waterloo Dock Entrance, Liverpool. She was built as the *Empire Farringay*, was renamed *Claire* in 1979 and was broken up at La Corunna in 1980.

Ingrid Gorthon (1952, 1,959grt) was owned by Stig Gorthon.

Voorspeler (1965, 854grt) was owned by African Coasters (Pty) Ltd and was built on the Clyde by Scott & Sons (Bowling)Ltd. In 1980 she was sold to New Boundary Shipping, Panama and in 1982 went to Uniship Lines, Panama and was renamed *Sagar*. In 1986 she sank off Banglabazar, India, and it was decided to demolish her there. This was completed on the 7 August 1988.

Cunard Line chartered Coast Lines *Pacific Coast* (1947, 1,188grt) in 1966 for a voyage to Tripoli, Libya.

Makalla of Coast Lines (1948, 1,265grt, 84m x 12m, 14 knots). Built as *Caledonian Coast*, she was renamed *Makalla* in 1967 and *Ahmadi Coast* in 1968. She was broken up in 1974.

Jacinth of Gem Line (1937, 651grt, 56m x 9m, 10 knots). She was broken up at Dalmuir in 1970.

Cory Maritime's *Pass of Dalveen* (1958, 965grt, 66m x 9m, 11½knots. She became the *Agbaraha-Otor* in 1972, *Barbara VII* in 1983 and the *Achilleas* in 1986.

Port Gentil of Soflumar (1953, 1,500grt, 78m x 11m, 11 knots). In 1980 she was sold and renamed *Mazal*, *Lacerta* and *Sunshield* in 1988. On 16 July 1988 her main engine was damaged and she was declared a constructive total loss. However, she was sold to Maltese owners and on 29 August 1989 was hit by gunfire north of Journieh, Lebanon. Ten crew died and she sank on 4 September.